SENSES

TASTE

Anita Ganeri

W
FRANKLIN WATTS
LONDON•SYDNEY

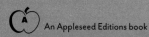
An Appleseed Editions book

Paperback edition 2017
First published in 2015 by Franklin Watts

© 2012 Appleseed Editions

Created by Appleseed Editions Ltd,
Well House, Friars Hill, Guestling,
East Sussex TN35 4ET

Designed and illustrated by Guy Callaby
Edited by Mary-Jane Wilkins

A CIP record for this book is available from the British Library

ISBN 978-1-4451-3256-3

Dewey Classification: 612.8'7

Picture acknowledgements
l = left, r = right, c = centre, t = top, b = bottom
page 1 siamionau pavel/Shutterstock; 2 iStockphoto/
Thinkstock; 3t Jupiterimages/Thinkstock; c and b iStockphoto/
Thinkstock; 4 Firma V/Shutterstock; 6t DenisNata/
Shutterstock; c and b l to r Hywit Dimyadi; DenisNata; Kati
Molin; Petr Malyshev; Pinkcandy/all Shutterstock; 7 Hemera/
Thinkstock; 8 Keith Brofsky/Thinkstock; 9 Nathalie Speliers
Ufermann/Shutterstock; 11 all Brand X Pictures/Thinkstock;
12 Jupiterimages/Thinkstock; 13 iStockphoto/Thinkstock;
14 wavebreakmedia ltd/Shutterstock; 15 Stockbyte/Thinkstock;
16 Kamira/Shutterstock; 17l fotohavran.eu/Shutterstock;
r BananaStock/Thinkstock; 18 Thinkstock; 19 Hemera/
Thinkstock; 20 Jupiterimages/Thinkstock; b iStockphoto/
Thinkstock; 21 Design Pics/Thinkstock; 22 Piotr Krze?lak/
Shutterstock; 23 David Evison/Shutterstock; image beneath
folios George Dolgikh/Shutterstock
Cover: Edward Lara/Shutterstock

Printed in China

Franklin Watts
An imprint of Hachette Children's Group
Part of The Watts Publishing Group
Carmelite House
50 Victoria Embankment
London EC4Y 0DZ

An Hachette UK Company
www.hachette.co.uk

www.franklinwatts.co.uk

Contents

Mmm, tasty

What happens when you lick an ice cream? What does it taste like?

Does the ice cream taste sweet or sour? Do you like the taste?

Taste is one of your senses. Your senses tell you about the world around you.

Your five senses are:

sight

hearing

touch

taste

smell

You see with your eyes

You hear with your ears

You touch with your fingers

You taste with your tongue

You smell with your nose

Favourite tastes

Look at these different foods.

They all have a different taste.

What is your favourite taste?

*There are lots
of different tastes
in the food we eat.*

6

Do you like sweet things, like milkshakes or cookies? Do you like salty things, like potato chips?

A milk shake tastes sweet because it has sugar in it.

How do you taste things?

You taste things with your **tongue**. Stick your tongue out and look in a mirror.

Your taste buds pick up different tastes in your food.

Your tongue is a lump of bendy muscle. It is covered in tiny bumps, called taste buds.

Taste bud places

Most of your taste buds are on your tongue. Some are inside your cheeks.

> **You have more than 10,000 taste buds.**

Your taste buds can tell you if your food tastes bitter, sour, sweet or salty.

Lemons taste *sour*

Potato crisps taste *salty*

Coffee tastes *bitter*

Jelly beans taste *sweet*

Taste messages

When you eat, your mouth makes spit. Tastes from your food mix with the spit.

When you see something tasty to eat, your mouth starts to make spit.

Your taste buds pick up tastes. Then they send messages about the tastes along nerves to your **brain**.

Taste and smell

Your senses of taste and smell often work together to tell you what your food is like.

If a cold blocks up your **nose**, you can't taste things properly.

Your food probably tastes like cardboard!

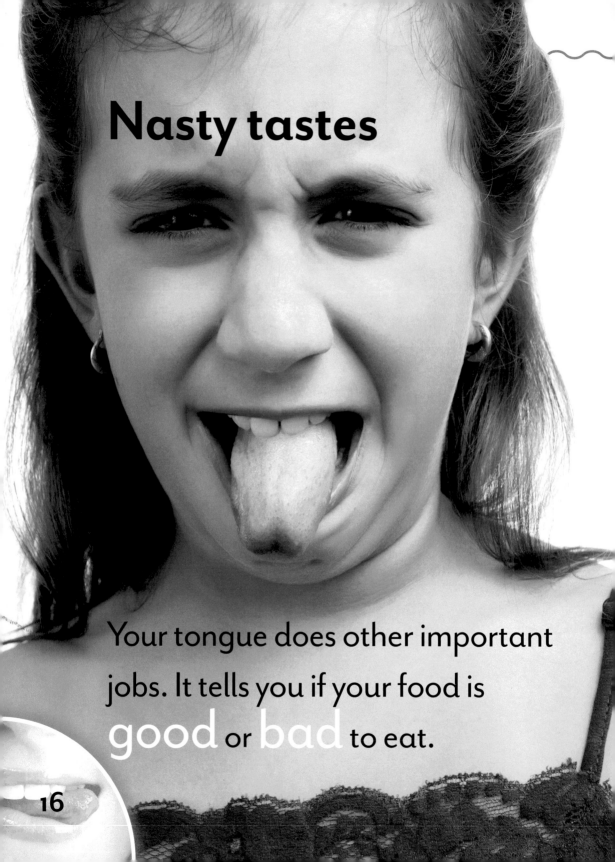

Nasty tastes

Your tongue does other important jobs. It tells you if your food is **good** or **bad** to eat.

Your useful tongue also tells you if your food is too hot to eat, or very cold.

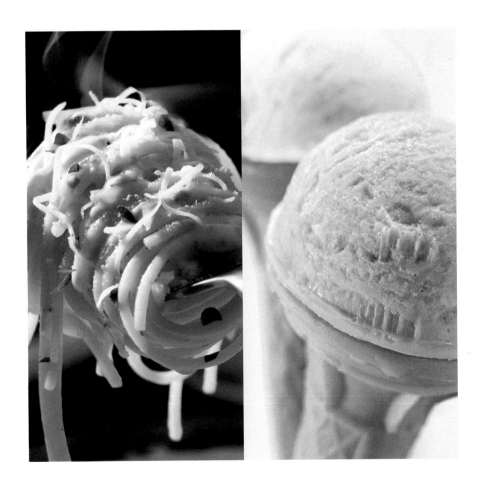

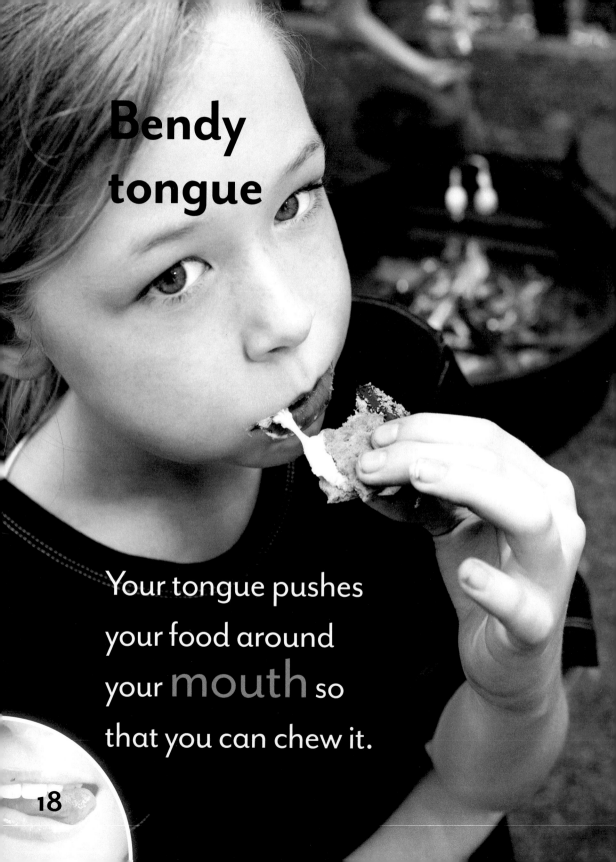

Bendy tongue

Your tongue pushes your food around your mouth so that you can chew it.

Then your tongue pushes your food to the back of your mouth so that you can swallow it.

Some things are easier to swallow if you drink some water.

Speaking out

Your tongue also helps you to make the sounds of words so that you can speak and sing.

To see how your tongue helps you to speak, press it down gently with your finger. Then try saying, 'Hi!'.

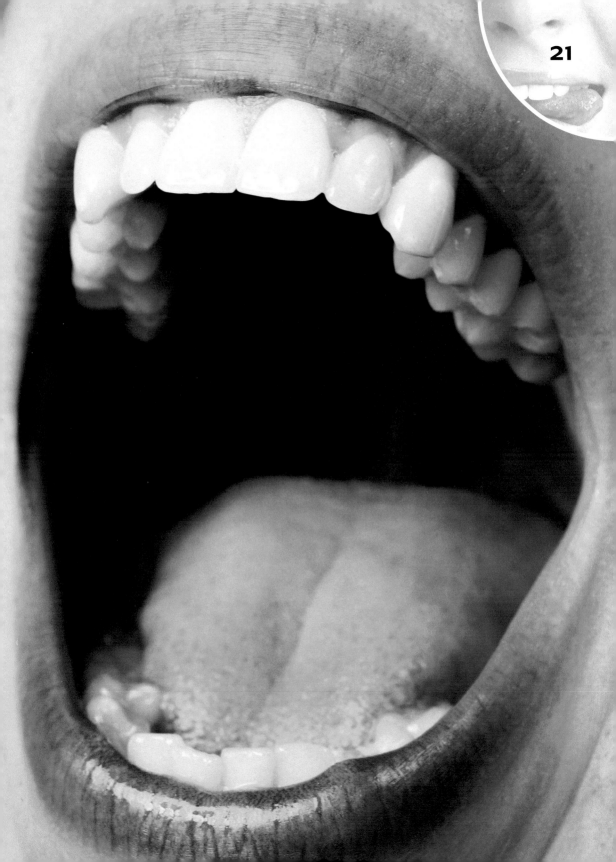

Taste facts

A butterfly tastes things with its feet. If it lands on a flower that tastes sweet, it uncurls its tongue and sucks up the nectar.

Your mouth makes about 1.5 litres of spit every day. Spit helps you to taste your food, and makes it easier to chew and swallow.

Giraffes have long, blue tongues that can be as long as your arm. Giraffes use their tongues for tasting... and for cleaning their ears!

Useful words

muscles
Parts of your body that help you move, breathe, taste and digest food.

spit
Watery liquid that you make in your mouth. Also called saliva.

nerves
Thin, long wires inside your body that carry messages between your body and brain.

taste buds
Tiny bumps on your tongue that pick up tastes in your food.

Index